Hole 5, We-Ko-Pa Golf Club page 41

SPECTACULAR GOLF
ARIZONA

THE MOST SCENIC AND CHALLENGING GOLF HOLES
IN THE GRAND CANYON STATE

Published by

PANACHE
PANACHE PARTNERS

Panache Partners LLC
469.246.6060
www.panache.com

Publishers: Brian G. Carabet and John A. Shand

Printed in Malaysia

Distributed by Independent Publishers Group
800.888.4741

PUBLISHER'S DATA

Spectacular Golf Arizona

Library of Congress Control Number: 2014954362

ISBN 13: 978-0-9886140-9-3
ISBN 10: 098861409X

First Printing 2016

10 9 8 7 6 5 4 3 2 1

Right: Phoenix Country Club, page 83

Previous Page: Emerald Canyon Golf Course, page 55

Panache Partners, LLC, is dedicated to the restoration and conservation of the environment. Our books are manufactured with strict adherence to an environmental management system in accordance with ISO 14001 standards, including the use of paper from mills certified to derive their products from well-managed forests. We are committed to continued investigation of alternative paper products and environmentally responsible manufacturing processes to ensure the preservation of our fragile planet.

SPECTACULAR GOLF
ARIZONA

INTRODUCTION

Just about everywhere on this planet, there are people drawn to a game that is impossible to get right. They are aware that failures might outnumber the successes, but they return time after time to participate in an activity that has become part of their life. Why do they do it? I posed this question once upon a time to a gentleman in charge of a course tucked away in a hard-to-find locale and his answer was immediate. "People play golf because of the land," he said. "Just look around you. It's peaceful. When you are on the course you forget about everything except golf. The scenery alone is worth the trip." And after decades of involvement in the sport, and taking into consideration the opinion expressed long ago by the gentleman at that out-in-the-country course, I have reached the conclusion that the land in the desert southwest of the United States is probably the finest in the world on which to build a course.

The classic courses in the eastern states, with their trees and hills, are obviously alluring. Any layout along the ocean has a certain advantage when it comes to looks. And the really big mountains clearly have a stark beauty that lures golfing patrons. In the desert, there is usually no single focal point on which to concentrate. The great thing about courses created in that unique landscape, however, is that the always gorgeous view is all encompassing. Everywhere you look there is the hearty vegetation that is not found just anywhere. As you play, you are surrounded by a stunning scene. Those scenes in all their beauty are found within the pages of this volume. The gorgeous photos come from golf courses in the region and in each case a hole from one of those courses is presented. They make up a tour of some of the area's most delightful, difficult, and decorative golfing attractions.

The automatic assumption of those who have never ventured into this part of the country for their golf is that one course in the desert will look pretty much like any other. That is certainly not the case. The Boulders looks nothing like the Emerald Canyon course. Jack Nicklaus said his Desert Highlands contained what he considered to be the greatest variety of foliage he had ever seen. And that course has a completely different feel than what is found at the Wildfire Golf Club, designed by Nicklaus' old rival Arnold Palmer. All of those courses appear herein and they represent just part of a trip that should be a treat for any and all who love the game.

Michael Rabun

Gold Canyon Golf Resort, page 107

CONTENTS

PAR 3

PAR 4

PAR 5

AK-CHIN
SOUTHERN DUNES
Golf Club

PAR 3 ◆ 165 YARDS

Maricopa, AZ
480.367.8949
www.golfsoutherndunes.com

Lee Schmidt and Brian Curley have become famous for creating uniquely stunning vistas that are the subject of countless photographs taken by bedazzled visitors. The fact that golf courses happen to wind their way through the gorgeous landscapes only adds to their fascinating work. They have helped spread golf in the Far East with their designs, and twice have been named the number-one golf architects in Asia. Schmidt and Curley, with assistance from World Golf Hall of Fame member Fred Couples, created the Ak-Chin Southern Dunes Golf Club course and it fits right in with their reputation for presenting something dramatic. Ak-Chin Southern Dunes consistently ranks among the nation's best public facilities and one glance at the wild beauty of the place shows why. Magnificent mounding and bunkering adorn the course, and examples of both can be found at the delightful, par-3 fourth.

It plays 165 yards from the very back of the tee box, but the six sets of markers and a shot of just 120 yards are all that are needed from the front. No matter which tee is selected, however, the view is intimidating, and an effort of reasonably high quality is required to escape the ever-present dangers. A sea of sand sits both in front of and behind the undulating green, so much so that the putting surface almost becomes an island. The bunker in front of the green is vast, beginning just in front of the teeing ground and containing sizeable pockets of native grasses. Two more traps are located behind the surface, and they in turn are set into miniature mountains of grass that pitch and roll like an angry ocean. Throughout the playing of Ak-Chin Southern Dunes, the task usually involves ignoring the views in order to concentrate on the shot at hand. On this course, that is never easy.

Photograph by Allan Henry

ANTHEM GOLF & COUNTRY CLUB

Ironwood Course

PAR 3 ◆ 217 YARDS

Anthem, AZ
623.742.6202
www.clubcorp.com/Clubs/Anthem-Golf-Country-Club

When it was decided that a second 18 holes was called for at Anthem Golf & Country Club, the man who designed the first course chose to give those who would play the new one a contrasting look. "I think it is every bit as nice as the first one (the Persimmon course)," designer Greg Nash said when the Ironwood course was opened. "But it definitely is different. We wanted a different look and feel."

The Ironwood layout is filled with risk-reward shots with 65 bunkers, many of them quite sizeable, and an array of seven water hazards. At the heart of the course is a stretch known to the membership as Anthem Alley, the opening three holes on the back nine that will usually make or break a round. The holes are played into the prevailing wind and consist of a par-4 with a peninsula green, a par-3 loaded with water, and a meandering par-5 that plays almost 600 yards from the back tee.

The middle portion of this test is a stern one-shot hole, the 11th, that can be played as far back as 217 yards. But from wherever the tee shot is struck it needs to be hit with authority. There is about 50 feet of open space in front of the green where the ball has a chance to bounce between the hazards, but everywhere else the water comes into play. One small pond protects the front-left portion of the green and another one wraps around the entire right and back sections. There are, as would be expected, multiple levels to the green to add to the examination. The Ironwood course can play from more than 7,200 yards down to about 5,400, so a player can find a challenge appropriate to the skill level. At no time, however, is anyone likely to suggest that Ironwood is a breeze.

Photograph by Jim Frenak

ANTHEM GOLF & COUNTRY CLUB
Persimmon Course

PAR 3 ♦ 199 YARDS

Anthem, AZ
623.742.6202
www.clubcorp.com/Clubs/Anthem-Golf-Country-Club

The design work of Greg Nash has steadily spread throughout the desert southwest, so much so that it can truly be said he knows the territory. Two of his most-praised works are found at Anthem Golf & Country Club north of Phoenix. The older, and somewhat more traditional of the two, is the Persimmon course. It is perhaps best known for a massive green of 18,000 square feet that sits hard by the clubhouse and serves as the finishing point for both the ninth and 18th holes.

There are plenty of other adventures awaiting, however, including a stretch of three holes early in the round that require all the attention a player can muster. The three-hole wake-up call begins with the par-3 second, which from the very back tee plays just a giant step less than 200 yards. There is enough water and sand scattered about to cause the intimidation meter to rise sharply, but it is a hole that does not require a forced carry as long as the correct shot is played.

For those hoping to put the ball close to the hole in a single shot, a high draw by the right-handed player is preferred. There is a tree placed short and right of the green that could easily impede such a shot, but that is perhaps the least of the problems associated with this hole. A lake sits to the right of the green and although it does not inch up to the edge of the putting surface it is still close enough to gobble up an errant tee shot. Another slightly smaller body of water wraps around the left and rear of the green and tends to come into play more than the one on the right. Bunkers are found eating into the front-left portion of the putting surface and awaiting behind the green. The next two holes are a twisty par-5 and a long par-4 that is the number one handicap hole on the course. It is a run of high-quality golf, the kind that brings an exhilarating challenge to anyone who loves the game.

Photograph by Jim Frenak

ARIZONA
Country Club

PAR 3 ◆ 197 YARDS

Phoenix, AZ
480.889.1505
www.azcountryclub.com

A golf course cannot be looked upon with high regard unless its putting surfaces are first rate, and those at Arizona Country Club have long been considered some of the best in the desert southwest. The greens have been pure since the PGA Tour's elite first stopped by to test them during the 1950s. And it is not just the fact that they are so smooth that sets them apart. Their design invariably grabs the player's attention, especially at the course's signature hole.

It is the par-3 11th, an almost 200-yard test that culminates a sensational two-hole stretch of golf. The preceding hole is a dynamite par-5 and the 11th is the longest par-3 on the course. On a layout where precise shots are called for from start to finish, none must be struck with more precision than the tee shot on this gem. It is actually possible to bounce the ball onto the green, but in order to do so the ball must hop through a gap of about 20 feet between a bunker and a lake that combine to seal off the vast majority of the front edge of the green. The water makes up the chief hazard on the hole since it will inhale just about any mis-hit shot. Beyond the green are two more bunkers, one of them housing two palms that emerge from the sand like oversized sentinels. Even if it takes more than one shot, the ball will eventually reach the green. And even though there is a collection of notable putting surfaces at Arizona Country Club, this one stands out. It has three distinct levels and is very close to 100 feet in width. If a shot comes to rest on one side of the green and the pin is placed on the other, much work remains before the task on this hole is completed. If multiple putts are required, at least there can be comfort in the fact that the ball is traveling over a pristine surface with picturesque views in the distance of both Camelback Mountain and the Papago Buttes.

Photographs courtesy of Arizona Country Club

THE BOULDERS CLUB
South Course

PAR 3 ◆ 187 YARDS

Carefree, AZ
480.488.9028
www.bouldersclub.com

The spectacular collection of rock formations that give The Boulders Club its name appear in a vast series of shapes and sizes. All of them have a singular appearance, but some are unique to the point that they have been given their own moniker. As you step to the seventh tee of the South course at The Boulders, for instance, the scene is dominated by a huge stone that balances atop the other. Known as Rosie's Rock, it is just one of the legion of geologic wonders that dot the landscape.

The golf at The Boulders, which comes in the form of 36 holes, is special as well. Rosie's Rock oversees a medium-length par-3 that involves a forced carry over a patch of desert to a green that wraps itself around a large bunker guarding the front-right corner of the putting surface.

A par is hard to come by if the tee shot finishes in that bunker, especially if it happens to wind up close to the lone but impressive cactus that resides in the sand. If a shot from the tee should get away a little to the left, there is a tree short of the green that can swat the ball down into an unattractive position.

The green is a two-level affair, and the back-right pin position turns the hole from a testy one into a sizeable challenge. And at the end of the hole comes, what else, another gorgeous formation of stone. The various tees for the eighth hole rest around and atop what is known as Promise Rock. Around every turn, there are adventures similar to the one the seventh hole presents, which is the reason The Boulders is such a special place to play.

Photograph courtesy of The Boulders, A Waldorf Astoria Resort

THE COUNTRY CLUB

at DC Ranch

13 HOLE

PAR 3 ◆ 128 YARDS

Scottsdale, AZ
480.342.7210
www.ccdcranch.com

The Country Club at DC Ranch in north Scottsdale offers an exclusive, yet inviting, lifestyle of social and sporting opportunities for couples, families, and professionals. The club reflects the history and charm of its beginnings as a desert cattle ranch in the early 1900s. Complemented by an unprecedented calendar of social events and activities for all ages, the club offers tennis, swimming, fitness, and an array of dining opportunities.

The course was redesigned by John Fought and Tom Lehman in 2002, and is traditional in style and features panoramic views. The 13th hole brushes right up against the spot where the McDowell Mountains begin their march upward. Fronted by desert, the 13th is the shortest of the par-3s at DC Ranch. A tee shot that is not much more than a short iron leaves no margin for error. The hole features an elevated tee and a green with bunkers to the left and behind. In between those features is the desert at its natural best and, for good measure, a rock wall runs around the front portion of the green to require a tee shot that is 100-percent carry. The green is surrounded by the beauty of the desert. Just as is the case on any other par-3, a well-struck tee shot and a putt of quality can produce a birdie. A birdie on this hole might carry a little extra weight when it comes time to leaf through your golfing memories. The previous and next holes run parallel with each other, with 50 foot elevation changes, one dramatically uphill, the other equally downhill. The 12th, a 260 par-4 is a potentially drivable par-4 or could call for a lay-up tee shot in the fairway leaving a short pitch to the slightly elevated green. The 14th, a 440-yard par-4, has out-of-bounds left, a hazard right, and a bunker seemingly in the middle of the drive zone; a tee shot down the right side of the fairway will bound to the bottom of the hill, leaving a pitch to the green. A great day at The Country Club at DC Ranch is to birdie two of the three mountain holes.

Photograph by Tony Roberts

EMERALD CANYON
Golf Course

5 **HOLE**

PAR 3 ◆ 147 YARDS

Parker, AZ
928.667.3366
www.emeraldcanyongolf.com

From the moment Emerald Canyon Golf Course opened in 1989, the word-of-mouth buzz was emphatic. The bottom line of that buzz was, "you have got to see this place." As time has gone by and the number of visitors has grown and grown, that buzz has only become louder.

The words "hidden gem" are perhaps thrown around too loosely, but they certainly apply to this unique course that sits hard by the Colorado River. The canyons, the huge boulders, the ups, the downs, the dramatically barren hillsides do not appear to be the best place to put a golf course. And yet one has been created that continually lures its fans back for another entertaining day of play.

Throughout the course there are views and holes that serve as conversation starters, and one of the most delightful is the par-3 fifth. Upon leaving the fourth green, players travel along the base of a mesa with the rock climbing almost straight up to the right

of the path that leads to the next assignment. That path makes a right-hand turn and suddenly there it is: a golf hole where logic suggests one should not be.

From the elevated tee, the green sits only about 145 yards away and the hole can be played much shorter than that. On the opposite side of a ravine there is a wide, shallow green that does not have a single bunker to act as guardian. Instead, the green sits down among the uplifted rock that pinches in to create a claustrophobic atmosphere. There is a small buffer of grass between the green and the forbidding landscape, but it takes only a slightly wayward shot to cause the ball to go bouncing off into some remote spot. It is even possible to catch a lucky bounce and have the ball carom off the rocks and back onto the green. Whatever the result, the experience of Emerald Canyon will be well worth remembering.

Photograph by Douglas E. Walker

FOREST HIGHLANDS GOLF CLUB
Meadow Course

PAR 3 ◆ 168 YARDS

Flagstaff, AZ
928.525.5200
www.fhgc.com

About a decade after helping put together the Canyon Course at Forest Highlands Golf Club, Tom Weiskopf returned to the scene and created a different style of golf. In the midst of a mountain pasture just north of the Canyon layout, Weiskopf designed what is fittingly known as the Meadow Course. The property is relatively flat, with ample room to drive the ball. Water comes into play here and there, the wildflowers add a colorful splash and, all in all, the course looks quite different from its hillier neighbor.

While there is a less confined feel to the Meadow Course, that does not mean the player can get away with just any old effort. Weiskopf was famous for producing crisp iron shots with his elegant swing, and just such a shot is called for at the par-3 eighth.

The approach at the previous hole requires a carry over a twisty little stream that connects two ponds, and one of those comes very much into play at the eighth. The view from the tee, in fact, consists of water and sand and then more water.

The pond all but envelops the hole, with the green forming a peninsula that sticks out into the hazard. If the tee shot is too short, it goes in the water. If it is too long, it goes in the water. If it sails left, it goes into the water. And if it goes right, there is a good chance it will finish in one of the two bunkers that squeeze up against the right front and right back of the green. The good news is that the hole is not a long one, so the player is not called upon to make a fantastic shot—just a good one.

Photograph by Kenneth J. Hamilton

GRAYHAWK GOLF CLUB
Raptor Course

PAR 3 ◆ 174 YARDS

Scottsdale, AZ
480.502.1800
www.grayhawkgolf.com

Four years after his best season on tour in 2003—including a win at the Masters—Mike Weir notched his eighth career victory at the Fry's Electronics Open contested for three years on Grayhawk's Raptor course (2007-2009). Raptor, one of two 18-hole layouts at Grayhawk, is considered among the finest public courses in the United States.

Tom Fazio designed Raptor to provide plenty of room off the tee, but a missed fairway usually results in a shot-making scramble to avoid a big number. The greens are large with a fair amount of undulation and tend to get a bit slippery as the Stimpmeter rises. The green at the par-3 eighth hole is a fine example of the challenges that Raptor brings to the table. This medium-length hole exemplifies the game's balance between challenge and beauty with native Sonoran Desert surrounding the hole and the magnificent McDowell Mountains framing the backdrop.

When it's time to pull the trigger, golfers first notice three front bunkers, which don't really come into play, and a large bunker to the right that guards the putting surface. A tee shot to the left portion of the green is recommended, not only to avoid the right bunker, but because the slope of the land falls decidedly from left to right. If the pin is located to the right, a shot to the middle has a good chance of working its way towards the hole.

A pin location on the left encourages players to favor that side of the green even more. In fact, they may consider landing the ball near the left fringe—allowing it to kick to the right off the slope and onto the putting surface. It is a thinking person's tee shot with the kind of puzzle that Weir was able to solve. Although not quite as prestigious as his major championship win, you wouldn't know it from the huge grin on his face as he hoisted the trophy on that Sunday afternoon.

Photograph by Lonna Tucker

GRAYHAWK GOLF CLUB
Talon Course

PAR 3 ◆ 175 YARDS

Scottsdale, AZ
480.502.1800
www.grayhawkgolf.com

Box canyons hold a special place in the history of the Old West after starring roles in countless movies as hole-in-the-wall hideouts for outlaws, improvised corrals for wild mustang roundups, or fine additions to already awe-inspiring landscapes. The back nine of the Talon course at Grayhawk Golf Club weaves its way around this wild and iconic symbol to provide an unrivaled desert golf experience.

The left side of the 10th falls away dramatically into an honest-to-goodness box canyon that also defines the primary challenge for the next hole—the par-3 11th. A gorgeous blend of nature and golf, this piece of ground is a dream come true for just about any golf course designer worth their salt. The tee boxes rise from the canyon floor with the special twist for those brave enough to take on the back tees.

As with every hole at Grayhawk Golf Club, the 11th has a name: "Swinging Bridge." On the way to the back tees, golfers must cross the hole's namesake to reach an

island of emerald-green grass perched above the canyon floor. Although the tee shot is much more manageable from the forward tees, golfers still must carry the chasm to be safe. A heavy-duty wood retaining wall backed by a gaping bunker mark the border between the canyon and the green complex.

The green is large and consists of two levels, front and back, with mounding all around and bunkers both left and right. These design elements combine to stoke the flames of anxiety, even among the most seasoned golfers. In the end, the tee shot at the 11th hole provides a white-knuckle moment within the entire Talon experience, one that players will remember regardless of the number they scratch onto the scorecard.

Photograph by Lonna Tucker

LAUGHLIN RANCH
Golf Club

Bullhead City, AZ
928.754.1243
www.laughlinranch.com

Those drawn to Laughlin Ranch Golf Club invariably comment about the vastness of the surroundings. In an area of the country where it is commonplace to feel overwhelmed by the natural wonders that press in from all around, this spot along the Colorado River ranks near the top in that regard. The golf course that serves as a recreational centerpiece to a growing entertainment complex provides all the challenges one would want, but it does so in a setting that can inspire as well as intimidate.

And inspiration can come in handy when tackling some of the challenges at Laughlin Ranch, among them the tee shot at the par-3 eighth. It is the longest of the short holes, one that can be played from as far back as 234 yards. But there are no gimmicks on this test—one plays a little downhill and fits like a glove into the encircling desert.

The path from tee to green sits on a grass-covered ridge that falls off on either side to the natural terrain and all the problems normally found on such land. At the end of that ridge is the target—a green that runs well over 100 feet in depth. It is another in a series of very large greens that make up one of the chief features of the course. During a trip around this layout, it is hard to avoid having at least one putt of monumental length. When standing on the tee of a par-3, the chore at hand often requires a sizeable forced carry over water or some other imposing hazard. At Laughlin Ranch's eighth hole, the chief concern is to hit a straight shot. Anything off to either side will find the desert and render a par all but impossible, unless some special inspiration can be gained from a glance at the nearby grandeur.

Photograph by Dick Durrance

OAKCREEK
Country Club

Sedona, AZ
928.284.1660
www.oakcreekcountryclub.com

There is a special combination in golf architecture that is hard to beat, and Oakcreek Country Club is fortunate enough to possess both parts: star power and a gorgeous setting. In the case of Oakcreek, the designers were golf giants Robert Trent Jones—both father and son. And the scenery is beyond magnificent, even by Arizona standards. Sitting among the geological features that make Sedona so unique, Oakcreek presents all the challenges expected from a quality course. However, the surroundings all but steal the show, and the fourth hole, which sits on the far western corner of the property, is a splendid example.

A straightforward tee shot to an elevated green that has bunkers placed on either side is imperative. There is no hazard to carry, no long grass with which to contend, no extraneous humps or bumps in the way.

Pines periodically dot the landscape around the entirety of the scene, but a shot would have to stray a great deal for any of them to become a factor.

What keeps the hole from being bland is the view that is common to all 18 holes at Oakcreek, but never so much as on this hole. A massive wall of rock, thrusting up from the ground and roughly hewn by the ages, creates a stunning backdrop to the hole. It is hard to concentrate on the golfing task when such overwhelming splendor is there for the viewing. Coming as early in the round as it does, the fourth hole presents a strong taste of what is to come as the course winds its way along the base of the rugged landscape that rises above it.

Photograph by Theo Andrusyszyn

OAKCREEK 13 HOLE
Country Club

PAR 3 ◆ 160 YARDS

Sedona, AZ
928.284.1660
www.oakcreekcountryclub.com

Water hazards are not in abundance at Oakcreek Country Club, but when they do come into play they are very much a factor. There is a pond near the clubhouse that can be particularly troublesome when playing the approach shot into the ninth. Another body of water protects the entire left side of the par-3 16th hole. And at the par-3 13th, one of the highlight attractions on this popular course, water combines with significant bunkering to make the tee shot the kind of challenge expected when playing a course originally designed by Robert Trent Jones Sr. and his son.

The 13th is not a lengthy hole, but when choosing between two particular clubs it is usually wiser to take the longer one. A shot that comes up short has an excellent chance of finding one of the four bunkers that are such prominent features of the hole. It is much easier to get up and down for a par if the ball hops a yard or two over the green than if a shot has to be played from the sand.

The water, however, is an entirely different problem. It comes in the form of a pond just left of the green and often acts like a magnet. The ground to the left of the green slopes toward the water, which is quite close to the putting surface. Two of the four bunkers on the hole sit between the green and the water and will often stop an errant shot from plunging into the hazard. Towering over the entire scene are the colossal walls of red rock that lure visitors to the region and create ever-present wonder. For those not used to such natural splendor, the sights surrounding Oakcreek Country Club more than make up for any wayward shots.

Photograph by Theo Andrusyszyn

THE PHOENICIAN GOLF CLUB
Desert Nine

8 HOLE

PAR 3 ◆ 120 YARDS

Scottsdale, AZ
480.941.8200
www.thephoenician.com

The northwest portion of The Phoenician and the southern base of Camelback Mountain are located so close together that there is almost no room between the two at all. As it turned out, however, there was just enough room to squeeze in one of the 27 holes of golf found at the AAA Five Diamond resort. This golfing experience is divided into the Canyon, Desert, and Oasis nines and provides one of the most memorable golfing treats in the Phoenix area.

The Desert Nine is likely the most popular of the courses because of its proximity to Camelback, one of the landmark attractions in an area filled with them. The fifth, sixth, and seventh holes run right along the base of the mountain and the seventh, a winding par-5, heads directly toward the resort itself. That brings you to the short eighth hole, which barely fits between the façade of the resort on the left and the slope of the mountain on the right.

The hole requires not much more than a pitch down the hill, and to reach the teeing ground a series of steps must be navigated. As many as eight tees are available and from some of them an enormous saguaro cactus partially obscures the view of the green. A large swale runs across the triangular green, a series of grassy mounds protect the front and right of the putting surface, and a lone bunker is located beyond.

The greens at The Phoenician are invariably well manicured and exceedingly quick; so much work usually remains once it comes time to putt. There are many golfing delights to be found at The Phoenician, but none can top the par-3 located along the lowermost slope of Camelback Mountain.

Photograph courtesy of The Phoenician

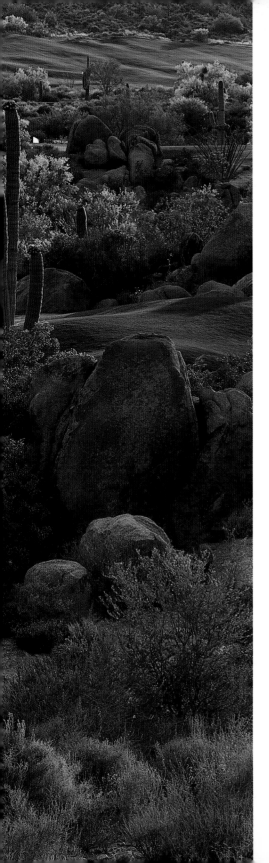

SUNRIDGE CANYON
Golf Club

PAR 3 ◆ 209 YARDS

Fountain Hills, AZ
480.837.5100
www.sunridgegolf.com

When confronted with a group of finishing holes called the Wicked 6, you know you're in for one of golf's great challenges. Designed by Keith Foster, SunRidge Canyon Golf Club's concluding stretch is particularly impressive and ultimately determines whether a golfer sinks or swims on this Sonoran Desert track. Hole 17 is certainly one-of-a-kind, even among this memorable closing half dozen, helping to wrap up the course like none other.

Starting off with a choice between two elevated teeing grounds—a championship tee on one side that plays 209 yards and a second championship tee that requires only 152 yards to the green—that little white ball will end up on the same green, but you'd almost never know it.

With a bunker in the middle and unique sloped surfaces on either side, the dual green creates a distinctive experience every time it is played.

The rest of this 6,823-yard, par-71 course is no less spectacular, boasting an authentic desert experience with tremendous mountain views and a prevailing breeze blowing down into the rugged canyon. At the heart of the round is the gradual descent into the canyon and then a subtle ascent back out, with a grand finale at the Spanish hacienda-style clubhouse for refuelling and relaxing.

Photograph by Lonna Tucker

THE LODGE AT VENTANA CANYON
Mountain Course

3 HOLE

PAR 3 ◆ 107 YARDS

Tucson, AZ
520.577.1400
www.ventanacanyonclub.com

Tucked into the foothills of the Santa Catalina Mountains, The Lodge at Ventana Canyon offers all the first-class comforts, activities, and dining choices one would want in a getaway spot—including two Tom Fazio-designed golf courses. *Golf Digest* recognizes Ventana as one of the top 75 golf resorts in America.

Although Ventana's two courses provide 36 holes of entertainment as they wind through the arroyos and elevation changes that make for such a dramatic backdrop, those who play at Ventana invariably come away talking about one particular spot on the landscape. And there is plenty of justification for them doing so. The par-3 third hole on the classic desert-style, target Mountain course is arguably the most photographed hole west of the Mississippi. It plays 107 exhilarating yards of cactus, canyons, and plunging ravines and invites you to take in a spectacular view of the Sonoran Desert terrain.

Fazio squeezed the hole into a corner of the mountains and created an instant conversation piece. From the second green, the path to the third tee climbs up to a peak. Once on the tee, the green becomes visible. It is tucked down among walls of rock with an army of cactus standing guard all around. The steeply downhill tee shot is only a few steps longer than 100 yards, so it is all about finesse rather than power. But the finesse must be just right. There is a rim of grass surrounding the undulating green, which usually plays fast, and a bunker is positioned off the front-right corner. Other than that, an off-target shot is likely to find a chunk of forbidding territory that has provided the subject for countless photos over the years.

Fazio could easily have created the Mountain course without the brief side trip into the rocky terrain. But he wanted to leave a special stamp on The Lodge at Ventana Canyon, and he was wildly successful in doing so.

Photograph courtesy of The Lodge at Ventana Canyon Club

WE-KO-PA GOLF CLUB
Cholla Course

5 HOLE

PAR 3 ◆ 207 YARDS

Fort McDowell, AZ
480.836.9000
www.wekopa.com

From the moment it opened early in the 21st century, the Cholla course at We-Ko-Pa Golf Club was hailed as one of the very best public layouts in the state and among the top 100 in the country. As designers have honed their skills with desert courses, the melding of the always-stunning surroundings with the turf grasses has developed into the kind of art form found at We-Ko-Pa. Architect Scott Miller proclaimed the site as, "ideally suited for a spectacular golf venue," and the par-3 fifth hole shows just what he was talking about.

It is a common theme with desert golf, but the views that are available often overshadow the manicured and maintained portion of a hole. Short holes have a chance to be the most stunning because nature can be brought closer to the action and nature is everywhere on this hole. Shrubs, bushes, and trees spring up from the rocky outcroppings, and a dry creek bed stretches across the front of the green.

The fifth at Cholla requires much more than a simple pitch shot from the tee, so the wash that must be carried is a formidable hazard. It is a classic example of a golfer having to take enough club for safety but facing plenty of problems if the tee shot travels too far. Grassy mounds have been built into the front corners of the green with the one on the left being the larger of the two. Any shot that lands on or around either of those mounds can bounce off into a very unfavorable spot. Two deep bunkers to the right of the green and another behind it create their own problems and the putting surface, itself, has multiple levels. It is the kind of visual treat one comes to expect in desert golf, and then some.

Photograph by Lonna Tucker

WILDFIRE GOLF CLUB
Palmer Course

PAR 3 ◆ 185 YARDS

Phoenix, AZ
480.473.0205
www.wildfiregolf.com

As his competitive record clearly shows, Arnold Palmer always seemed at home when playing golf in the desert southwest. He was a threat to win anywhere he played, but he seemed to be especially dangerous in the kind of environment found around Phoenix. Three of Palmer's 92 professional wins came in the Phoenix Open, and they were won in succession beginning in 1961. It was fitting, therefore, that he designed one of the two courses attached to the JW Marriot Desert Ridge Resort & Spa, which is just 17 miles from downtown Phoenix.

The Palmer course at Wildfire Golf Club provides 18 holes of adventure, filled with tumbling fairways, sizeable greens, and the starkness of a surrounding landscape filled with native vegetation. A splendid example of desert-style golf at its finest can be found at the eighth hole, one that demonstrates a par-3 does not need lots of water to be an excellent test. The ground surrounding the green pitches and rolls with varying degrees of severity, so if the tee shot does not land on the putting surface it may bounce off one of the slopes and offer a challenging up-and-down.

The hole can play between 135 and 225 yards to the middle of the green. The green itself is fairly narrow, but quite deep. That puts a premium on club selection, because if the pin is placed at the back of the green and the ball winds up on the front, a putt of considerable complexity will await. When playing the eighth on the Palmer course, accuracy is well advised.

Photograph by Golf Shots Unlimited

AK-CHIN SOUTHERN DUNES

Golf Club

14 HOLE

PAR 4 ◆ 323 YARDS

Maricopa, AZ
480.367.8949
www.golfsoutherndunes.com

A truly great short par-4 usually gives the player choices. If the wrong choice is made, a severe penalty often must be paid. Lee Schmidt and Brian Curley built a dandy at Ak-Chin Southern Dunes Golf Club, a course heavily laden with bunkers that are uniformly troublesome. Staying out of the sand becomes the chief objective when playing Ak-Chin Southern Dunes, and that assignment reaches its zenith at the par-4 14th, which from the middle set of tees plays right around 300 yards. Length, therefore, is not a factor at this hole and putting the ball into the fairway off the tee is simplicity itself.

An iron may be all that is needed to loft the ball into the ample landing area that sits in the midst of as much sand as one would ever want to see on one hole. A bunker runs along the entire right side of the 14th and oozes out into the fairway before being replaced by a group of traps that surround the green.

The primary feature of the hole, however, is found to the left of the fairway. It is here that a huge mound plays host to a nest of bunkers. If the player has the distance to carry that formidable hazard, it is possible to reach a sanctuary of short grass that sets up a mere short pitch to the green.

Only those with a long game and a taste for recklessness will attempt to fly the ball over this out-of-the-ordinary obstacle. A safe play off the tee can bring about an approach shot in the 100-yard range to a green that is tucked behind uplifted earth. Each hole at Ak-Chin Southern Dunes carries a name, and the moniker for the 14th is Beautiful Surroundings. The surroundings, indeed, are eye-catching, but a better name for this gem might be Safety First.

Photograph by Allan Henry

AUGUSTA RANCH

Golf Club

PAR 4 ◆ 293 YARDS

Mesa, AZ
480.354.1234
www.augustaranchgolf.com

A growing trend in the world of American golf is the creation of what have become known as executive courses. They are shorter in length, with the aim of reaching an audience that might not otherwise be drawn to the game. If there is a desire to play a round of golf in less time than it would take on a regulation-sized course, then an executive layout provides that opportunity. Such courses are springing up all over the country as part of golf-oriented communities, and there is one on the eastern edge of Mesa that has been honored as the best such layout in the state.

That course is Augusta Ranch Golf Club, which plays to a par of 61 and reaches out to families, juniors, and anyone else who wants to experience golf. But don't be fooled by the shorter length. The course also presents its share of challenges, including a short par-4 that would be a welcome addition anywhere the game is played.

The 12th hole measures just under 300 yards and its chief features are the three bunkers that are placed in a line: the first one short and right of the green and the other two close by the putting surface. At some point these bunkers must be taken into consideration when determining the proper path to the green, which sits in the midst of subtle mounding that adds a special touch to the task at hand.

Just because an executive course might be shorter than some of its cousins does not mean it is bland or easy to conquer; a trip around Augusta Ranch will make that fact abundantly clear.

Photograph courtesy of Sharon Dennis

THE COUNTRY CLUB
at DC Ranch

6 HOLE

PAR 4 ◆ 451 YARDS

Scottsdale, AZ
480.342.7210
www.ccdcranch.com

The sixth hole at The Country Club at DC Ranch is one of the more challenging, signature par-4s on the course. The hole measures 451 yards from the back tees and 369 yards from the forward tees. From the back tee it is as demanding as any hole on the front nine. Off the tee on this seemingly straight par-4, there is a 40-yard landing area of grass that banks slightly right to left. On the left side of the fairway are two large bunkers that keep your ball from bouncing into a deep wash running parallel with the hole and just beyond the desert.

If you land in these bunkers, you are forced with a 200-yard shot on to the green. A monster drive needs to negotiate a fairway bunker on the right side of the fairway at about 320 yards.

The hole gets feisty as the approach is to a 5,000-square-foot green with as much movement and slope as any green on the course. A short second shot will not bounce on as there is a slight mound protecting the front of the green, which has no surrounding bunkers.

The green slopes toward the back fringe, so any ball hit beyond the center of the green will go over the back of the green. So an accurate second is a must. Any player is pleased to par this hole and scurry on to hole number seven. The sixth is by far the most demanding par-4 on the front nine.

Photograph by Tony Roberts

DESERT FOREST
Golf Club

PAR 4 ◆ 435 YARDS

Carefree, AZ
480.488.4589
www.desertforestgolfclub.com

Desert Forest Golf Club has earned the reputation of being the first true desert course in the country and is quite simply a classic. It is golf in its most basic form and has drawn accolades of the highest sort since its opening more than half a century ago.

Desert Forest has become an even more alluring attraction since it underwent a 21st-century update in 2013. It is easy to see why many view this as their favorite course in Arizona. The course fits as neatly into the landscape as any one you will find. The desert and all its hazards nestle close to the fairways, there is not an out-of-bounds stake anywhere, there are no fairway bunkers, and there is nary a water hazard. When it came time for the reconstruction project, all of the greens and their surroundings, including the bunkers, were made anew. It is a new course with the same classic look and the same routing of holes.

Desert Forest has lots to choose from when it comes to standout holes, but the 15th is as good as any. It is a relatively short par-4 that runs straight as a string to the green. A forced carry is required off the tee, but it is not all that far and the glories of the desert vegetation that must be dealt with only add to the gorgeous nature of the hole. There is a prominent mound in front of and to the left of the tee, cactus make an occasional appearance, and the fairway rolls and sways. Ultimately, the view must be ranked right up there with any to be found in the sport. The second shot is to a slightly uplifted green protected by two bunkers on the right and one on the left. The ball can be run up onto the green if needed, something the old-school followers of the game insist should be possible. Finally, Black Mountain can be clearly seen beyond the green—off in the distance but always making its presence felt.

Photograph by Corinne Paringer

DESERT HIGHLANDS

PAR 4 ◆ 406 YARDS

Scottsdale, AZ
480.419.3745
www.deserthighlandsscottsdale.com

When Jack Nicklaus set about to design his highly acclaimed Desert Highlands course, he made the observation that the property contained, "probably a greater and denser variety of desert foliage than I have ever seen." All of that plant life alone made for a dazzling spot on which to place a golf course. The sizeable elevation changes around the layout and the imposing presence of nearby Pinnacle Peak only added to the special nature of the place. Blending the desert with the fairway and greens is the chief goal of any architect who works in this part of the world and Nicklaus is a master at it.

The par-4 10th is as good an example as any on the course, a hole that begins from the side of Prospector Mountain, in the shadow of Pinnacle Peak and drops into a fairway that has been neatly sculpted out of the surrounding native vegetation. It is not a long hole, and the ample landing area lined by mounds of grass on either side provides a target that is relatively easy to find.

As with Nicklaus courses around the world, however, things grow a little more complicated when it comes time to approach the green. Between the middle of the fairway and the putting surface is a wash of sand, grasses, and prickly plants that forces a shot from the upper reaches of a player's talent level. The waste area reaches the front edge of the green and hillocks of grass rise and fall around the other three sides of the surface to create an awkward pitch for those who are overly cautious in their bid to avoid the desert.

Soon after it opened, the course was deemed a perfect setting for the made-for-TV Skins Game. Nicklaus was joined by Gary Player, Arnold Palmer, and Tom Watson for those friendly battles. They played a course that rewarded golfers with a timeless beauty that serves as a perpetual lure to one of Nicklaus' finest designs.

Photograph by Evan Schiller

EMERALD CANYON
Golf Course

PAR 4 ◆ 297 YARDS

Parker, AZ
928.667.3366
www.emeraldcanyongolf.com

The must-see and must-play Emerald Canyon Golf Course has become a destination for the devoted golfer for obvious reasons. It is fun to play, it is great to look at, and since it's a county-owned facility it is easy on the pocketbook. The course plays to a full distance of 6,437 yards and that, by 21st-century standards, does not pose an ominous threat. But the surrounding mountainous terrain and all of its accompanying crevices and outcroppings make for the sort of hazards that are far more entertaining to deal with than pure length.

At number seven, for example, only 297 yards need to be traversed to reach the flagstick. It is obvious from the tee, however, that they will be 297 of the most adventurous yards one will ever play. The hole runs between a pair of foothills that represent the start or finish of the nearby mountains—depending on which way a person is heading.

Those mountains run down to the Colorado River, which is less than 300 yards from the seventh green. From an elevated tee, a shot must be played between the walls of rock to a fairly narrow fairway that bends to the left. A series of hearty trees cling to the base of the rock outcroppings along both sides of the fairway, but if the trouble can be avoided with the tee ball, the second shot will obviously not have to travel too far. Three bunkers are placed short of the green, one of them running across the face of the putting surface. The uplifted rock that is such a feature of this hole runs around behind the green, creating the kind of distraction that is commonplace on this course.

Like so many of the holes at Emerald Canyon, the seventh is not long. But it is dramatic to an extraordinary degree and is one of the many reasons this course has become so much of an attraction.

Photograph by Douglas E. Walker

EMERALD CANYON

Golf Course

PAR 4 ◆ 283 YARDS

Parker, AZ
928.667.3366
www.emeraldcanyongolf.com

Since the beginning of time, man has been fascinated and lured by the stories of hidden treasure. Such a treasure can be found near Parker, Arizona, at a place referred to as the "Jewel in the Desert" but better known as Emerald Canyon Golf Course. The memorable course is carved out of the mountains and canyons overlooking the Colorado River.

Emerald Canyon is a four star-rated golf course, according to *Golf Digest*, which describes the course as "an unexpected pleasure with a fantastic, unusual layout and stunning surrounds." In fact, Emerald Canyon was selected as the "Best Exotic Course in Arizona" by *The Arizona Republic*.

There are six lakes on the course, several of which are also used as habitats for two endangered local fish species: the razorback sucker and bonytail chub.

Emerald Canyon was named Conservationist of the Year by the American Fisheries Society, uniquely adding to its reputation as a special golf experience.

Upon leaving hole 15, you travel up a mountain path wondering if you will ever arrive at the top. The tee box of hole 16 is one of the highest spots on the course, featuring a beautiful 360-degree view of the mountains and the Colorado River. Your tee shot must carry a ravine of approximately 140 yards. On the opposite side of the ravine, you are hitting onto a "green" surrounded by railroad ties, true to the character of a Pete Dye design. A fairway bunker comes into play from the elevated tee box and a greenside bunker often comes into play on your approach shot. The view from the 16th is so spectacular that Emerald Canyon has hosted weddings on the tee box.

Photograph by Douglas E. Walker

THE ESTANCIA CLUB

2 HOLE

PAR 4 ♦ 389 YARDS

Scottsdale, AZ
480.473.4400
www.estanciaclub.com

Given a reasonable piece of ground on which to put down a golf course, designer Tom Fazio will invariably create a masterpiece—after all, no modern-day golfing architect has more courses listed among America's top 100 than he does. So when given acreage to work with that is as spectacular as that found alongside Pinnacle Peak in north Scottsdale, breathtaking results were expected. Sure enough, The Estancia Club ranks among the nation's best. The views alone create an incredible experience, as the course travels up and down through the beauty that is the Sonoran Desert.

One of the early tests gives an example of the playability of a Fazio design. The second hole is a short par-4, one that can play from about 300 yards to almost 400 depending on which of the six tees is chosen. As with every hole at Estancia, the second is surrounded by the stunning scenery of the desert, boulders, and various forms of cactus abounding.

The fairway makes a turn to the left and the line off the elevated tee is a distant bunker on the outside corner of the dogleg. A drive that finishes on the right side of the fairway will provide the best angle into the green, which is narrow in front and wide in the back. Two bunkers protect the entire left side of the putting surface and another smallish one is placed alongside the right front corner. Off in the distance Scottsdale is visible, offering a tempting distraction. A birdie opportunity could be in the offing early in the round, but as is commonplace throughout Estancia, the vista more than makes up for a score that is not up to par. The second is the first of three wonderful short par-4s at Estancia.

Photograph courtesy of The Estancia Club

THE ESTANCIA CLUB

13 HOLE

PAR 4 ◆ 411 YARDS

Scottsdale, AZ
480.473.4400
www.estanciaclub.com

The Tom Fazio-designed Estancia Club has become renowned for its gorgeous surroundings as much as for the world-class nature of the golf itself. Those two elements blend together over the course of 18 memorable holes, and the par-4 13th demonstrates how the natural and manmade elements of the layout come together seamlessly.

One aspect of Estancia that is appreciated the more it is seen is the flow of the land. The contours can almost be taken for granted, but they are an integral part of the design and should be appreciated just as much as the amazing views. The 13th is a straightaway hole and the longer the tee shot, the narrower the fairway becomes.

The second shot is the key; it is here that there should be an appreciation for the way the ground is shaped. There are no homes in sight and you have a view of Pinnacle Peak. With two bunkers that pinch in at the left side, the green's unique shape allows for a variety of pin placements. Those bunkers become even more of a factor when the hole is cut in the back-left portion. The 13th tee is considered by most members to be the most beautiful tee at Estancia.

Photograph courtesy of The Estancia Club

THE ESTANCIA CLUB

18 HOLE

PAR 4 ◆ 462 YARDS

Scottsdale, AZ
480.473.4400
www.estanciaclub.com

During the first 17 holes of a golfing experience at The Estancia Club, it's easy to feel overloaded by all there is to see. And then comes a final explosion of natural beauty that more than rivals everything that has come before. Set among miniature mountains of rock, boulders, and natural vegetation is the 18th of a Tom Fazio-designed course that holds its spot amidst America's best.

From an elevated tee there is abundant room in which to place a drive. It is the right side of the fairway, however, that offers the more favorable approach to the green. Five bunkers are located left of the fairway for about the final 100 yards of the hole. The green is not very wide, but it is quite deep and sits adjacent to an outcropping of rock.

The only bunker associated with the green is a small one off to the right against the rocks, and is there more for definition purposes than for gathering in wayward shots.

Each hole has its own special view, whether an isolated bit of scenery associated only with that spot or something of a grand scale that can only be described as panoramic. The view from the 18th tee is one that will be remembered long after the round. Clearly, Tom Fazio has saved the best for last.

Photograph courtesy of The Estancia Club

PAR 4 ◆ 403 YARDS

Fountain Hills, AZ
480.836.8100
www.firerockcc.com

There is a singular peak on the eastern edge of the Valley of the Sun known as Red Mountain, a unique outcropping that reaches almost 3,000 feet above sea level. When the light is just right, the rugged formation appears to be on fire and thus this jagged formation has taken on the nickname "firerock." That nickname has been transferred to various nearby entities, including the FireRock Country Club—the first private club built in the city of Fountain Hills.

FireRock takes full advantage of the surrounding terrain and vistas while offering a delightful series of holes carved out of the natural landscape. Very early in the round, there is a classic example of what the course is all about. There are a number of holes at FireRock played from an elevated tee, and one of those is the par-4 third. The back tee is located partway up one of the many slopes that run through the course and from there it is possible to see downtown Phoenix.

Red Mountain itself is visible far beyond the green. It is a straightaway hole, although the fairway makes a slight twist to avoid a set of three bunkers that creep in from the left. Long hitters must make sure they do not get caught up in the sandy hazards, but no matter the distance of the tee shot a left-to-right ball flight will be preferred. That will create the best angle to play away from the chief trouble on the hole—a pond to the right of the green and the two troublesome bunkers that sit between the putting surface and the water. The water hazard is well below the surface of the green, and the bunkers are accompanied by mounding that can only add to the difficulty if an untimely bounce creates a grassy lie and an awkward stance. There is a mix of golf and scenery abounding throughout the region, but FireRock provides one of the best of those combinations.

Photograph by Eric Kruk

FOREST HIGHLANDS GOLF CLUB
Canyon Course

9 HOLE

PAR 4 ◆ 466 YARDS

Flagstaff, AZ
928.525.5200
www.fhgc.com

Tom Weiskopf has noted that mountain courses pose special challenges but that the dramatic views are worth the extra effort. Weiskopf should know, since he has designed plenty in up-and-down terrain, one of his more spectacular projects being the Canyon course of Forest Highlands Golf Club, designed in conjunction with Jay Morrish.

The vistas are stunning, the golf is first class, and at the heart of the course is a gem of a hole. It is the 9th, a stout par-4 that spreads through a magnificent amphitheater with walls of pines on every side. One of those pines is the chief feature of the tee shot, standing all by itself on the right side of the fairway. From the elevated tee, the best line is one that takes the ball right over the tree. That allows the player to avoid the small stream that trickles along left of the fairway, as well as the bunker that waits on the left side of the landing area.

A solid tee shot, however, is just the start. The creek eventually makes a right-hand turn and runs across the fairway before turning into a full-fledged pond. There is room to the left of the pond in which to bail out, but in order to put the second shot into the middle of the green the water must be carried. The green itself is elongated, thus providing a variety of pin placements, and is protected on either side by bunkers. At the back of the green is a narrow strip of putting surface that travels up and over a hump and connects the putting surfaces of both the ninth and 18th holes. It is a complex and beautiful hole, just the kind one would expect from a master designer who has been given a unique landscape on which to demonstrate his skills.

Photograph by Tony Roberts

GRAYHAWK GOLF CLUB
Talon Course

PAR 4 ◆ 416 YARDS

Scottsdale, AZ
480.502.1800
www.grayhawkgolf.com

When David Graham won the 1981 U.S. Open at Merion Golf Club, his final round was acclaimed as one of the finest ever played in a major event. His tee-to-green precision resulted in a 3-under-par 67 that pushed him from three shots behind to three shots in front. In the sunset of his playing career, Graham joined forces with golf course designer Gary Panks to create the Talon course at Grayhawk. The duo stitched some of their finest work into Talon's layout with Graham's propensity for precision leading the way.

As is true with many of the holes on Talon, the fairways appear a bit tighter than they actually are with subtle swales and thick Sonoran Desert concealing the true breadth of the landing areas. The par-4 16th is no exception. At 416 yards, it demands a reasonable amount of length with an extra measure of precision to avoid the desert flanking both sides. Those who find the fairway are granted several options, while those who don't are wise to chop it out to the short grass.

Left pin placements bring a large bunker into play that begins about 80 yards from the putting surface and loops around to the front-left corner of the green. The back-left section of the green is higher than the front-right with a ridge running between them that may be used as a backstop for short-right pin locations. If the hole is cut in the back, however, golfers must pull an extra club and bring it in high with some spin to avoid running off the back, leaving a quick downhill, down-grain third shot.

Talon's 16th hole certainly personifies the type of precision that made Graham a major champion, but it's also clear that he and Panks had an eye for aesthetics, too. This becomes apparent while peering down the 16th fairway to see green ribbons of grass crowned by Scottsdale's majestic Pinnacle Peak in the background.

Photograph by Lonna Tucker

LAS SENDAS
Golf Club

PAR 4 ◆ 450 YARDS

Mesa, AZ
480.396.4000
www.lassendas.com

Las Sendas Golf Club was the first course in Arizona produced by Robert Trent Jones Jr. And the course he built will test every aspect of a player's game—patience included. Las Sendas has turned into one of the most respected layouts in the region. Thought must be brought into play on every shot and when the proper play has been decided upon, it is recommended that the game plan be executed to near perfection.

Only the most skillful should tackle the course from the silver tees, which provide almost 7,000 yards worth of trouble. But from one of the more forward of the six available tees, the strategic nature of the course can be enjoyed to the fullest. A golfer does not ease into the action at Las Sendas. From the opening shot it is apparent that this is not going to be a pushover. The opening hole provides all anyone would want in the way of a challenge, what with the water, sand, rolling fairway, diabolical green, and ever-present desert to be conquered or avoided.

It is a hole that would be a spectacular finishing hole on any championship layout, but at Las Sendas it serves as a wake-up call.

The first hole makes a hard dogleg to the right around a pond that stretches from just in front of the teeing ground almost all the way to the green. Two fairway bunkers can come into play, especially a devilish trap that sits in the middle of the fairway near the inside corner of the dogleg. The green complex is particularly intriguing with a troublesome trap sitting in the slope that leads up to the putting surface. Another huge bunker awaits behind the green, buried in an enormous mound that rises up to dominate the scene. It is a wide, shallow green with a hump running from front to back that creates two separate sections of short grass. This hole makes it clear that if challenging golf is what you are after, you have come to the right place.

Photograph by Lloyd B. McBean

LAS SENDAS

Golf Club

10HOLE

PAR 4 ◆ 467 YARDS

Mesa, AZ
480.396.4000
www.lassendas.com

The initial Arizona design work presented by Robert Trent Jones has grown in stature since Las Sendas Golf Club opened late in the 20th century, and those with professional skills have come to recognize it as a "second shot golf course."

Every phase of the game is tested at Las Sendas, but the shots into the greens are almost always challenging. None more so than at the par-4 10th, a wonderful example of desert golf that pleases the eye in addition to putting demands on one's skills. The back nine begins with a tee shot that is straightforward, directed to a reasonably ample landing area. A waste area must be carried from most of the six tees that are in play on the hole and even though the fairway is fairly wide, things can become quite hazardous in a hurry if that fairway is missed. The desert vegetation, tall and thick, creeps right up to the edge of the short grass and presents plenty of problems if the tee ball travels in an improper direction.

It is the second shot, however, that makes this hole. A series of ridges and mounds in the fairway can complicate the stance for the second shot, but the biggest difficulty rests with an enormous bunker that sprawls across the front of the elevated green. That trap must be avoided if par is to be considered a likely goal. A bail-out area is available to the right of the trap, but that brings about an uphill pitch shot that must be ultra precise in order to save a four. Two more bunkers protect the left side of the green and there is another one beyond the putting surface, but it is the big fellow in front that makes or breaks a score at the 10th. A heroic second shot is required on this hole, and it will make for one of those special golfing memories.

Photographs by Lloyd B. McBean

MESA
Country Club

10 HOLE

PAR 4 ♦ 417 YARDS

Mesa, AZ
480.397.9000
www.mesacountryclub.com

Mesa Country Club boasts one of the most venerable courses in the state of Arizona, one that was designed by a pioneer of American golf course architecture and whose name is attached to one of California's historic layouts.

The course has been lengthened through the years but it maintains its traditional, parkland feel. It has some old-time quirks in that a few of the holes are played over a road and others traverse a canal. The set of par-3s have a delightful variety, the greens are small, the fairways are lined with enormous trees, and, all in all, Mesa Country Club has the look and feel of a course that has been around a long time— which it has. Another defining feature of the course is that half the holes sit along the edge of the mesa that gives the city its name.

William "Billy" Bell designed the course in 1948, having had a hand in creating Riviera Country Club in suburban Los Angeles. There is even a hole at Mesa that resembles one at Riviera, where the PGA professionals compete each year. The teeing ground for both Mesa's 10th and Riviera's first are in the shadow of their respective clubhouses and the opening shot on both travels sharply downhill to the landing area below. The 10th at Mesa is a challenging par-4 that is not particularly long but is quite narrow. The trees that are so much a factor throughout the course encroach on both sides at hole 10 and two perfectly placed bunkers narrow the landing area. Two more, smallish bunkers sit at the front corners of the green. It is a straightforward hole that does not involve a lot of flash. But like the rest of this very respected course, it requires solid golf.

Photograph courtesy of Mesa Country Club

OAKCREEK
Country Club

6 HOLE

PAR 4 ◆ 370 YARDS

Sedona, AZ
928.284.1660
www.oakcreekcountryclub.com

Focusing on what a particular shot requires at Oakcreek Country Club is always difficult because of the constant distraction brought about by the scenery, but concentration is certainly needed when it comes time to take on the par-4 sixth hole. Accuracy off the tee is a must and the proper trajectory for the second shot is also called for. The hole fits the design theme of the late Robert Trent Jones Sr., who, along with his equally famous son, laid out the Oakcreek course with the philosophy that "every hole must be a hard par and an easy bogey."

The tee shot at the sixth is struck from a chute of trees, and additional trees are a factor down both sides of the fairway. Anything from the tee that strays from the intended path could easily leave a player blocked for the second shot, which is difficult enough without having a large obstacle in the way.

From the fairway, the mammoth formations of red rock that make this course so visually unique loom off to the left. For the approach to the green, however, it is best that the player pays more attention to the sand that must be avoided than to the geological formations.

There are three large bunkers attached to this hole and one of them sits directly in front of the putting surface. The biggest of the traps is located short and right of the green and another is found just beyond that one. Any mis-hit shot from the fairway or one that has too much left-to-right action increases the likelihood that a sand wedge will have to be brought into play. Saving par from one of the traps will be problematic, just as the elder Jones always said it should be.

Photograph by Theo Andrusyszyn

PARADISE VALLEY
Country Club

PAR 4 ♦ 407 YARDS

Paradise Valley, AZ
602.840.8100
www.paradisevalleycc.com

Paradise Valley Country Club carries a well-deserved reputation for being a top-of-the-line establishment, no matter what brings guests and members to its facility, and that is especially true when it comes to golf. The Lawrence Hughes-designed course, which has been in operation for more than half a century, contains all the subtle challenges found in classic layouts. It is not a course that pummels the player with forced carries and penal hazards that can spoil a round in a split second. Instead, there is classic feel of old-fashioned golf. That does not mean the course is a pushover. Far from it. Quality shots are required at Paradise Valley just as they are at any other high-profile course, but it becomes obvious from the very start that this is a place for those who love the game in its purest form.

There is no finer example than the eighth hole, a straightaway par-4 that places the utmost premium on accuracy. The tee shot is one of the most demanding on the course with a pond to the right of the fairway and a row of eucalyptus trees running down the left. One of the features of Paradise Valley is the uplifted nature of the greens and the eighth is raised slightly from the surrounding turf. The last of the trees pinches in from the left just short of the green, which means a drive down the right side of the fairway is preferred. Naturally, that brings the water into play—one of the many examples of the strategic nature of the course design. A bonus to the second shot is that nearby Camelback Mountain serves as a very impressive backdrop. There are mounds built into the green, although they are not the kind that pitch and roll to a major degree. Instead they are the kind that tend to baffle the player with their confusing breaks. A bunker protects each of the front corners of the green and they are best avoided if a par is to be expected.

The more an old-style course is played, the more it is likely to be appreciated. Such is the case with this golfing jewel that oozes tradition.

Photograph by Tony Roberts

PARADISE VALLEY
Country Club

9 HOLE

PAR 4 ◆ 371 YARDS

Paradise Valley, AZ
602.840.8100
www.paradisevalleycc.com

Although golf has made all the advancements one would expect in today's technologically-oriented society, the sport's roots are still placed deep in tradition. And for those who yearn for golf the way it was once designed to be played, Paradise Valley Country Club presents the perfect retreat.

It is a course that rewards not only the good shot, but the one to which thought has been given. Placing the ball in the proper location was a major part of golf in previous generations. Doing so remains an asset at Paradise Valley.

The front nine finishes with three strong par-4 holes, and the ninth is a lovely example of the kind of golfing architecture that prevailed in the middle of the 20th century. At the close of the front nine is a par-4 of well under 400 yards from the back tee, but one that will give players all they want. A well-designed short par-4 usually calls for a tee shot into a narrow space and then requires an extremely precise approach.

After all, if distance is not required then accuracy should be. The tee ball at the ninth must avoid the trees, which line the left side of the fairway and serve as a dividing line between the first and ninth holes. There is a slight dogleg to the left and where the fairway makes the bend, two bunkers dramatically reduce the size of the landing area. And then comes the fun part. Although traps are a chief feature of Paradise Valley, the ninth green is the most well-bunkered on the course. A huge trap has been placed in the face of the slope leading up to the green and travels from the right-front corner of the putting surface all along the right side. Four more bunkers run around the back and left sides of the green. It makes for something of an elevated island green that also has two tiers. The double-leveled green only adds to the complexity of a hole that is a standout attraction on a standout course.

Photograph by Tony Roberts

PHOENIX
Country Club

PAR 4 ◆ 460 YARDS

Phoenix, AZ
602.263.5208
www.phoenixcountryclub.com

Phoenix Country Club is one of Arizona's original and most historic clubs, located in the heart of downtown. The club originated in 1899 and has been located at its current site since 1927. Senator Barry Goldwater's brother Bob, known as "the father of the Phoenix Open," was instrumental in the Phoenix Open's creation in 1932, where it remained at the club through 1986. One of the oldest events of the PGA Tour, it has been host to many legends of the game. Players on the course today are able to enjoy its storied past and see it through the eyes of such greats as Ben Hogan, Byron Nelson, Arnold Palmer, and Jack Nicklaus.

A course re-design took place in 2002 by Tom Lehman and John Fought, who agreed that preserving the old-school style was of the utmost importance. The 18-hole course features year-round playability as well as stunning views of Piestewa Peak, Camelback Mountain, and the downtown Phoenix skyline.

Kicking off the back nine, the 10th hole is perhaps the most challenging on the course. The 460-yard dogleg left is guarded in the driving area by a large bunker on the right and trees on the opposite side. Once the player has found the fairway, a middle- to long-iron approach must be carefully played to a large elevated green guarded by bunkers on the front left and right side of the green. A score of par-4 is a welcome sight to anyone's scorecard.

Photograph courtesy of Phoenix Country Club

TROON NORTH GOLF CLUB

Monument Course

PAR 4 ◆ 299 YARDS

Scottsdale, AZ
480.585.5300
www.troonnorthgolf.com

When designing a short, risk-reward par-4, there is a delicate balance that must be achieved for the hole to be truly worthwhile. The opportunity for reward needs to real. It is not worth the risk, after all, if the chance for success is so small that it is not worth the trouble.

Former British Open champion Tom Weiskopf is likely unsurpassed in the world of golf architecture when it comes to creating a true risk-reward hole and one of his very best can be found on the Monument course at Troon North Golf Club. The 15th hole measures only 299 yards from the very back, and if the safe route is chosen there is a considerable amount of fairway on which the tee shot can be placed. But what about those who wish to have a go at the green with one, big blow? Weiskopf has given that kind of player a reasonable chance for triumph. A solid shot with perhaps a hint of draw for the right-handed player can actually run up on the green as long as it can scoot between the strategically placed bunker short and right of the putting surface

and all the native landscape that awaits on the left. If an attempt at a heroic shot goes considerably awry, however, any one of the many hazards associated with desert golf can wreck havoc with the scorecard. If it is a risk-reward hole, after all, there does have to be some risk involved. An enormous outcropping of boulders dominates the scene beyond the back-left corner of the hole, and even when the elongated green is reached the work is not yet finished because of the rolls and swales that come into play on long putts. It is clearly not a long hole and when quality shots are combined with caution, a par can be expected. The fun comes, however, when caution is put aside. And at Troon North, Weiskopf has created a hole where the potential for reward makes it quite tempting to take the risk.

Photographs by Jay Jenks

VERRADO 13 HOLE
Golf Club

PAR 4 ◆ 310 YARDS

Buckeye, AZ
623.388.3000
www.verradogolfclub.com

It often happens in desert golf that a remote piece of ground appearing on the surface to be inhospitable to the sport is turned into a jewel of a playground. British Open champion Tom Lehman and U.S. Amateur winner John Fought combined to create just such a course in the extreme western portion of the Phoenix metropolitan area. It is Verrado Golf Club, sitting at the base of the White Tank Mountains and consisting of a blend of styles. The front nine has a links look and the back nine creates a more classic desert feel. The course has been on *Golfweek's* prestigious "Best Courses You Can Play" list for several reasons, the most obvious one being that it is a fun place to swing a club.

One of the most fascinating challenges comes at the 13th hole, a short par-4 which the very longest of drivers might consider taking on with one, mighty blow. But such a strategy, even for those who hit the ball a truly monumental distance, is not advised. The temptation for something heroic is made greater once it becomes obvious that

there are no bunkers and no water hazards for the entire distance of the hole. The green, however, is a small one and the pitches from around the putting surface are filled with peril. On top of that, the hole plays decidedly uphill. A smooth swinging layup shot, therefore, is the play for just about everybody. Such a tee shot, one that leaves 100 yards or so, will bring about an approach that gives the average player a chance to pull off the kind of result that could be the talk of the post-round meal. The second shot, however, is not a piece of cake. The green, built into a point where the ground rises up to create the mountains, presents its own test. There is a false front that must be carried and the green has two tiers. It is very advisable to put your second shot on the tier where the hole is located or three putts will become a very likely occurrence. Verrado's 13th hole looks peaceful from the tee, but thanks to the design work of Lehman and Fought, it can turn nasty in a hurry.

Photograph by D2prod.com Murphy/Scully

WILDFIRE GOLF CLUB
Palmer Course

PAR 4 ◆ 410 YARDS

Phoenix, AZ
480.473.0205
www.wildfiregolf.com

No matter where or when a golf course is built, the roots of the game can be unearthed if the architect cares to do so. Arnold Palmer has leaned heavily on the roots of golf in his work at Wildfire Golf Club. Just as it was when the game was first played, the lay of the land is often the chief hazard on Palmer's course at the JW Marriot Desert Ridge Resort & Spa.

The par-4 12th is perhaps the chief example. There is not a single bunker on the hole, which makes a gentle left-hand turn with subtle rises and falls all along the way. An accurate tee shot is necessary to put yourself in position to attack a very challenging green. A small group of trees must also be negotiated, which are bunched together on the right edge of the fairway a little less than 100 yards from the green. But most of the action comes on and around the green itself.

The putting surface is a multi-level affair; surrounding the green are humps and hollows that would look right at home on a course in Scotland or Ireland.

What makes this hole unique, however, are the collection areas around the green. If you go long, you are chipping downhill to a difficult green. Short shots must stay clear of a 20-foot-wide mound that starts about 60 feet short of the green and gets wider as it goes. If an approach shot ends up left or right of the green, a delicate chip shot must carefully negotiate the undulating green to the correct tier. A score of par is always a win on this hole.

Photograph by Golf Shots Unlimited

AK-CHIN SOUTHERN DUNES

Golf Club

PAR 5 ◆ 584 YARDS

Maricopa, AZ
480.367.8949
www.golfsoutherndunes.com

For the most part, there is plenty of room in which to place a shot at the visually dramatic Ak-Chin Southern Dunes Golf Club. That, naturally, is a good thing because of what is to be found in the places where the green grass is not growing. Ak-Chin Southern Dunes, another in a series of truly astonishing works from the design team of Lee Schmidt and Brian Curley, is as unforgiving as it is beautiful. As with any other course in which intimidation plays a key role, the ability to focus on the upcoming shot is vital. If the swing does not quicken and the mechanics are sound, reasonable results should be expected.

The par-5 seventh at Ak-Chin Southern Dunes gives the player a very good chance at a satisfying result. Two solid shots can set up a not-so-long approach to a green that, like most on this course, is a well-protected target. To start with, the tee shot needs to avoid a menacing bunker down the right side that stretches out for close to 70 yards.

There is plenty of room to the left of the trap in which to place the tee ball, although eventually the grass stops and the desert begins. The second shot's landing area is narrower than the first's, and a bunker that pinches in from the left is the chief obstacle. It is a simple matter of choosing the proper line and making a smooth swing.

The approach shot must carry two bunkers that are built into an upslope and partially hide the green. Another bunker is found beyond the surface, which itself is full of tilts and swales. Ak-Chin Southern Dunes is a course that presents its hazards clearly and boldly, thus telling the player, "Don't hit it here." That, as it turns out, is advice worth following.

Photograph by Allan Henry

ARIZONA
Country Club

PAR 5 ◆ 503 YARDS

Phoenix, AZ
480.889.1505
www.azcountryclub.com

The annual PGA Tour stop in the Phoenix area has been contested since 1932, and on 10 occasions Arizona Country Club was host to the event. Arnold Palmer won on the course twice and so did Gene Littler. Billy Casper was a winner at Arizona CC, as was Julius Boros. In addition to being in the World Golf Hall of Fame, all of those players won the U.S. Open and it took a player of the highest caliber to challenge for the title when this venerable course welcomed the game's best. When Littler won the Phoenix Open in 1955, he did so with a score of just 5-under par. That was on a course that in those days measured less than 6,300 yards. In 1963, The Big Three finished 1-2-3 for the first time ever in a PGA tour event or major championship with Palmer trumping his fellow Hall of Famers Gary Player by one and Jack Nicklaus by two.

The combination of tree-lined fairways, a wealth of bunkers, and occasional water features brings about the need for exact shotmaking.

Nothing less than that is called for at the par-5 third, where an early round risk-reward challenge is faced. In addition to the typical narrowness of the tee shot, the one at the third has the added feature of a boundary down the left side and a pair of bunkers at the outside corner of the dogleg. A layup is a long way from easy due to a large tree that encroaches along the left side of the fairway and a lake that also pinches in from the left for the final 140 or so yards of the hole. Finally, there is a kidney-shaped green with the water sitting just to the left and a bunker sweeping across the front of the large, undulating putting surface.

It is the kind of hole that must be thought through and on which proper execution is a must. The kind of hole, in fact, found in abundance on the U.S. Open courses conquered by the legendary players who also managed to win at Arizona CC.

Photographs courtesy of Arizona Country Club

ARIZONA
Country Club

10 HOLE

PAR 5 ◆ 593 YARDS

Phoenix, AZ
480.889.1505
www.azcountryclub.com

Arizona Country Club is well into its second half century with a storied history and a traditional-style course that when played from its full distance provides all the golf anyone would want.

Especially the opening hole on the back nine, a full-blooded, three-shot, par-5. Even from the forward tees, the 10th is a potential blow up hole. But from the tips, from where the hole stretches to just a few steps short of 600 yards, it calls for three solidly struck, precise shots just to have a chance to put a five down on the scorecard.

The hole runs pretty much straight away, angling the slightest bit to the right after the tee shot. With such a long way to go, that tee shot needs to land safely in the fairway—which means avoiding the two bunkers that sit to the right of the intended landing area. After reaching the proper location off the tee, the second shot must squeeze its way into a narrow section of short grass between a bunker on the left

and a collection of towering palms on the right that can easily impede the intended path to the green. As if getting into position for a straightforward third shot was not troublesome enough, the approach itself presents its own share of difficulties with a lake encroaching to the very edge of the green across the entire front and right side, just waiting for a crisp wedge shot to zip backwards into the drink. For those with fear in their hearts, the two bunkers to the left and long were perfectly positioned to grab the shot that is struck with an extra amount of safety built into the game plan.

During its distinguished tenure on the region's golfing scene, Arizona Country Club has become known for its requirement of high-order shot making skills. Nowhere does that hold true more than it does at the 10th, which certainly holds its own among the most challenging par-5s in the nation.

Photographs courtesy of Arizona Country Club

ARIZONA GRAND
Golf Course

PAR 5 ◆ 538 YARDS

Phoenix, Arizona
602.431.6480
www.arizonagrandresort.com

Although there are plenty of places in the desert southwest to simply let go and have fun, Arizona Grand Resort & Spa is hard to beat. There are the rooms, of course, plus the massive water park, dining opportunities galore, and miles and miles of hiking trails that wind through the adjacent South Mountain Park—all 13,000 acres of it and advertised to be the largest municipal park in the United States. And then, there is the golf.

From start to finish, Arizona Grand Golf Course offers memorable views and memorable shots; a wilderness experience in an urban setting. Of the myriad dramatic moments that will be a part of any round at Arizona Grand, the most out-of-the-ordinary one will come at the par-5 13th. Few holes are more visually intimidating. The desert waste on both sides of the fairway contains humps and crevices, bunkers and vegetation. Only after hitting two solid shots into a narrow landing area, however, can the most frightening feature of the hole be fully appreciated.

The green sits well above the level of the fairway, and built into the slope leading up to the putting surface are three enormous bunkers. They have been created in stair-step fashion with only a sliver of grass located between each of the imposing traps. The first of the three is about 70 feet wide and is the biggest. But none of them are any bargain, and they all must be carried with the steeply uphill approach shot. The green begins 15 yards or so from the back of the final bunker and the surface, which is not all that wide, stretches almost 100 feet deep. So it is not just a matter of successfully carrying the shot to the green up and over the bunkers. The hole location must also be taken into consideration when trying to figure out which club to use.

There are lots of things to see and do at Arizona Grand Resort & Spa, but for the golfers, the most unique experience will likely involve the stunning 13th hole.

Photograph courtesy of Arizona Grand Golf Course

BLACKSTONE
Country Club

9 HOLE

PAR 5 ◆ 555 YARDS

Peoria, AZ
623.707.8710
www.blackstonecountryclub.com

Jim Engh has developed into one of golf architecture's shining lights, creating courses around the world and building individual holes that look more like portraits than they do playing fields. His first Arizona project is Blackstone Country Club, a hideaway outside Phoenix named for the black volcanic outcroppings that make periodic appearances in the landscape. For those who appreciate minimalist design work, Blackstone is a classic.

The course is not overwhelmed with bunkers—some holes have none at all. The greens vary, with some wide and shallow and others narrow and deep, and the mounding that surrounds many of the greens is stunning. As with other Engh products, Blackstone provides a golfing experience with enough twists and turns to make it a one-of-a-kind treat. The front nine comes to a close with a par-5 that only the most skillful and long-hitting players will think about attempting to reach in two mighty blows.

A tee shot into an ample landing area needs to avoid the lone bunker on the hole, which has been placed on the outside corner of the fairway as it makes a turn to the right. The second shot must carry a native area into another wide spot in the road. The fun part comes next; the green sits beyond a boulder-filled ravine and is loaded with undulations throughout its 60 feet in width. It is a shallow green, but the right side is more so than the left. The ground rises steadily behind the green with a combination of rock, manicured grass, and trees, and sitting above it all is the clubhouse, which resembles nothing short of a castle-fortress. A very bold look indeed, and coming from an architect who has a tremendous flair for the dramatic.

Photograph courtesy of Blackstone Country Club

THE BOULDERS CLUB
South Course

5 HOLE

PAR 5 ◆ 545 YARDS

Carefree, AZ
480.488.9028
www.bouldersclub.com

There is an area in the northern reaches of the metropolitan Phoenix area that amounts to a theme park for geologists. Volcanic and earthquake activity from many millions of years ago created rocks that range in size from enormous to gigantic. Each collection of stone seems to be more stunning than the previous one and in the midst of all of this has been built a world-class resort along with 36 holes of challenging golf. The complex is known, naturally, as The Boulders, A Waldorf Astoria Resort. And it represents one of the best vacation destinations in the nation.

The largest of the rock formations sits near the main building of the resort and directly behind the green at the fifth hole on The Boulders Club's South course. From the tee of the par-5 hole, there is no doubt where you are headed. Just aim for one of the most easy-to-spot golfing targets on earth—a soaring mass of stone that finds itself constantly posing for photos. In addition to being placed in such an uncommon setting, the fifth hole presents a high-quality test.

The tee shot can either be carried over a wash filled with desert vegetation or played out to the right to an island of fairway that provides sanctuary. Those with a high degree of skill or those using one of the forward tees will likely attempt to reach the main fairway, from where the second shot is a straightforward, uphill layup to a fairly generous landing area. Bunkers to the right and beyond protect a green that sits close to some of the casitas that house guests of the resort.

But from start to finish, and particularly at the finish, the focal point of this hole is the monumental collection of rock that dwarfs the surroundings. Some of the uppermost pieces of the formation look for all the world as if they are ready to become dislodged, which would create quite a disruption in the pace of play. Through the course of time, however, the geological wonder has remained as is, allowing the action to continue and creating a perpetual sight to behold.

Photograph by Sammy Todd Dyess

DESERT MOUNTAIN CLUB

Cochise Course

18 HOLE

PAR 5 ◆ 511 YARDS

Scottsdale, AZ
480.595.4318
www.desertmountain.com

Desert Mountain Club presents a one-of-a-kind opportunity for golfing overload. There are six courses, all of them designed by Jack Nicklaus. On top of that, the Desert Mountain Cochise course was the host for 13 years to The Tradition—one of the five major tournaments on the Champions Tour. Nicklaus won the tournament four times, joining World Golf Hall of Famers Raymond Floyd, Lee Trevino, and Tom Kite as champions on the Cochise layout. As Desert Mountain was being brought to fruition, Nicklaus said its creation had been, "one of the highlights of my career as a golf course designer." The Cochise course has been spotlighted more than any of the other layouts on the vast property because of its history as a major championship test. It features an island on which two greens are located, for the seventh and 15th holes.

There are five fabulous par-5s at the Cochise, including one that serves as the concluding hole of the round. The 511-yard, 18th hole is reachable in two for the big hitters, but only at the risk of winding up in the desert, a prepared bunker, or both. A vast majority of those who play the hole, of course, will treat it as a three-shot challenge and the chief task for each of the first two shots will be to stay out of the natural landscape that is filled with trees, bushes, and the small, prickly plants that grow in massive abundance. The approach to the green must carry a dry wash inhabited by a lone tree that can easily come into play if the pin is located on the right side of the putting surface. It is a wide and fairly shallow green fronted by a pot bunker. A much larger trap guards the left portion of the green and an even larger bunker loaded with vegetation will absorb any shot that carries long.

The 18th on the Cochise course is made for championship play and the unique thing about Desert Mountain is that there are 107 other holes that have the same quality.

Photograph courtesy of Desert Mountain Club

FLAGSTAFF RANCH
Golf Club

PAR 5 ♦ 536 YARDS

Flagstaff, AZ
928.226.3111
www.flagstaffranch.com

Standing on the 18th tee at Flagstaff Ranch Golf Club recalls former U.S. Open Champion Jerry Pate's golf design philosophy: "If we choose, we could build golf courses to torment the greatest players in the world," he said. "But challenging doesn't have to mean fierce. A golf course should be a place to relax, enjoy time with friends, and escape the pressures of today's fast-paced world." That is the kind of course Pate put together at Flagstaff Ranch, one which scales the sizeable elevation changes and drifts through the Ponderosa Pines. Some of those magnificent trees line the left side of the par-5 18th hole, a delightful test that provides options all along the way.

A bunker located along the right edge of the fairway is pivotal because it signals the start of a lake that travels along the right side for the final 200 yards. If the tee shot is struck with the intention of getting past that bunker, it had best be a precise one, because the fairway narrows dramatically beyond the bunker.

A tee ball that stays short of the lake leaves a second shot that must deal with another strategic bunker, one that eats into the fairway from the left and leaves only a smidgen of room between the sand and water. Whether to challenge that bunker with the second is another important question.

The green itself is protected by two bunkers and the water on the right, and a large bunker off the front-left. A ridge runs across the green, making it advisable to put the approach shot on the same portion of the green where the hole has been cut. As is Pate's desire in his design work, the 18th hole at Flagstaff Ranch is not meant to be fierce. Worthwhile shots, however, are still needed to achieve the desired amount of fun and excellent shots are rewarded.

Photograph by Pamela Ott

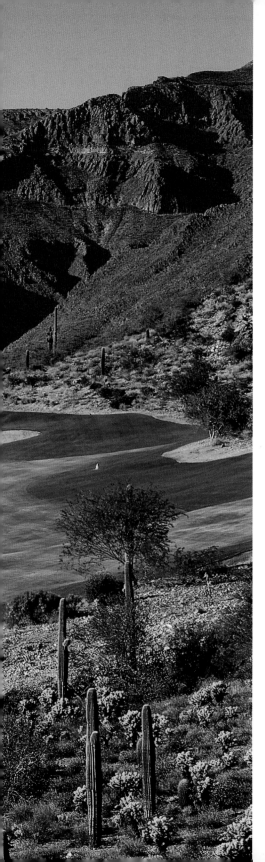

GOLD CANYON GOLF RESORT
Dinosaur Mountain Course

3 HOLE

PAR 5 ◆ 514 YARDS

Gold Canyon, AZ
480.982.9090
www.gcgr.com

The Dinosaur Mountain course at Gold Canyon Golf Resort is consistently rated one of Arizona's top public golf courses. In fact this hidden gem was voted by an American sports magazine as one of the top 10 "underrated" courses in the nation. High praise, indeed, and one trip around the gorgeous terrain will make it clear why the course receives such accolades.

Unforgettable certainly describes the Dinosaur Mountain course, where the championship layout is laced with a rollercoaster ride that would rival Six Flags. Elevation changes abound. One of those comes on the par-3 fifth hole, which drops dramatically to a green that is divided by a swale. That challenge comes at the end of a magnificent three-hole stretch that serves as the backbone of the course. It all begins with the par-5 third, a

dramatic dogleg up the namesake mountain that earns its spurs as Gold Canyon's signature hole.

With legendary Superstition Mountain looming in the background, the tee shot must carry over a vegetation-filled wash to an elevated and sloping fairway. Other than the forced carry and the ravine on the left, the chief hazard off the tee is the lengthy bunker that protects the inside corner of the dogleg where the fairway makes a sweeping turn left. Longer hitters can try to go for it in two but the smart play is to lay up 80 yards short of the green. Finally, if all has gone well to this point, a short uphill pitch remains to the ultimate target—a long, narrow, two-tiered green that sits in a distinct saddle.

Photograph by D2 Productions

LAS SENDAS
Golg Club

18HOLE

PAR 5 ◆ 576 YARDS

Mesa, AZ
480.396.4000
www.lassendas.com

It is the goal of any golf architect to make a course's concluding hole a memorable one, and Robert Trent Jones, as he has been prone to do in his career, succeeded at Las Sendas. His initial project in Arizona is laden with holes that provide all the golf one might ask for and the 18th is certainly one of those.

The 18th winds around and between two bodies of water and concludes with a green that sits between the sort of bunkers and mounds that are such major features of the course. The first order of business is to squeeze the tee shot into the sizeable landing area, a section of fairway that sits at the spot where the hole makes the first of its two turns. A pond on the right side of the fairway looms as the chief hazard off the tee, after which the hole angles sharply to the right. Another water hazard, taking up more space than the first one, appears to the left of the fairway and comes into play not only for the second shot but also for the approach to the green.

The ideal landing spot for the second shot is a fairly level area that sits amid the many rolls found along the rest of fairway and once in this location a shot of about 80 to 100 yards is left. There is a narrow passageway onto the green between the water and a deep, multi-pronged bunker that guards the front, right portion of the putting surface. Beyond the green, the ground runs down into a bunker and then back up to form a mound that overlooks the scene.

The 18th at Las Sendas is easily playable as long as the shots are the kind that a player hopes to produce. The intimidation factor, however, is sizeable and leaves the kind of memories expected from a high-quality finishing hole.

Photograph by Lloyd B. McBean

LAUGHLIN RANCH
Golf Club

2 HOLE

PAR 5 ◆ 650 YARDS

Bullhead City, AZ
928.754.1243
www.laughlinranch.com

The spot where Arizona, Nevada, and California meet once ranked among the more forbidding locations in the United States, but old-fashioned American free enterprise can overcome just about anything. Where there was once desolation, there are now places to live, shop, and be entertained. Visitors pour into the area and those with golf on their mind automatically head to Laughlin Ranch Golf Club.

The course, designed by David Druzisky among the gorgeous arroyos that make up the desert foothills alongside the Colorado River, is panoramic in nature. The wide expanse of the vistas tends to make some of the holes look larger than they really are, and most of them are plenty large to begin with. Take the second hole, for instance. It measures a colossal 650 yards from the extreme back tee, although this expansive par-5 can play as short as 475 yards. The fairway is wide, rolling, and seemingly never ending. The hole invites the player to rare back and let loose with a full-blooded

strike and then to do so again. Two bunkers appear within the confines of the fairway over the second half of the hole, and the ground drifts upward as the green nears. Off in the distance the Black Mountains serve as an imposing backdrop.

The greens at Laughlin Ranch are uniformly large and have the sort of sizeable undulations that match the broad scope of the landscape. Everything about the place is big. Laughlin Ranch is located in Bullhead City, Arizona, but it takes only a few minutes to negotiate the roads that travel past the airport, over the Colorado, and into Laughlin, Nevada. That is where the casinos are located, serving as a type of recreation quite different from the golf. Together, the game of chance and the game of skill have turned this once barren locale into an oasis.

Photograph by Dick Durrance

LOEWS VENTANA CANYON

Canyon Course

PAR 5 ◆ 503 YARDS

Tucson, AZ
520.577.1400
www.ventanacanyonclub.com

Featuring 36 holes designed by Tom Fazio, Loews Ventana Canyon offers a challenging and memorable experience. Immersed in the beauty of the lush desert foliage, the property is home to an abundance of wildlife—deer, roadrunners, quail, rabbits, and birds. Ventana's courses are defined by unique layouts and stunning views of the Sonoran Desert and Santa Catalina Mountains. They wind through spectacular canyons, sloping arroyos, and saguaro cactus forests.

The Canyon course is designed around the inspiring beauty of the Esperero Canyon and incorporates the massive rock formation known as Whaleback Rock. Showcasing a partial green and a cascading waterfall, the signature 18th is a par-5 of comfortable length, giving long hitters a chance to pull off the enjoyable feat of reaching the green in two mighty blows. As expected, however, there are complications awaiting those who try and fail to get home in two. Challenges involve the narrowness of the fairway and the hazard that crosses in front of the green in the form of a rock-strewn ravine.

Trees line both sides of the fairway and a cactus-filled bunker pinches in from the left to complicate matters. Those playing the 18th as a three-shot hole—and they would be in the vast majority—must again contend with the trees to find a proper spot for the approach to the green. If two solid hits have properly negotiated the rolling fairway, a reasonably short shot is left to a green that serves as just a part of a beautiful view.

To the right of and beyond the large green is a sizeable, two-layer water feature. Not only does the water make up a gorgeous architectural creation, it comes very much into play for the approach to the green. An imposing stone wall serves as a dam for the upper level of water and beyond that is the entrance to the resort itself, a massive structure built from native stone with the look of a 21st-century fortress.

Photograph courtesy of The Lodge at Ventana Canyon Club

WE-KO-PA GOLF CLUB
Saguaro Course

PAR 5 ◆ 515 YARDS

Fort McDowell, AZ
480.836.9000
www.wekopa.com

The products of the design team of two-time Masters champion Ben Crenshaw and Bill Coore have become some of the most talked about courses on the planet, so it was not surprising their services were sought to create a second layout at We-Ko-Pa Golf Club. They did not disappoint.

The Saguaro course is a wonderful complement to the Cholla course, which was the original layout at We-Ko-Pa. Although there is no escaping the fact that the 18 holes sit in the middle of some of the most exquisite desert scenery to be found anywhere, Saguaro often takes on the feel of a links course. Fairway bunkers pop up from time to time just as they do on the seaside courses in Scotland. The fairways themselves are laden with links-like ripples. It is a tribute to golf of yesterday, when most of the trouble was off to the side and could be avoided by a straight shot that did not need to be hit majestically high. At the par-5 eighth, for example, the hoped-for result can be achieved with simple, pure golf, something Crenshaw and Coore favor.

The imposing cactus that give the course its name are all around, of course, the unmistakable profile of Red Mountain soars off in the distance, and a wayward shot can still find the abundant, rugged wasteland on which the course sits. On this hole, however, the chief hazards along the way are the bunkers that make periodic appearances along either side of the fairway. Of all those bunkers, the most noticeable one is the wide expanse of sand that oozes its way into the left side of the fairway about two-thirds of the way along the hole. There is a trap short and right of the putting surface and three more guard the sides, but the approach shot can be run onto the green.

Crenshaw and Coore have created a course that is perfect for the golfing public that plays it, one with traditional features built in an out-of-the-ordinary setting.

Photograph by Lonna Tucker

WILDFIRE GOLF CLUB
Faldo Course

HOLE 15

PAR 5 ◆ 594 YARDS

Phoenix, AZ
480.473.0205
www.wildfiregolf.com

Nick Faldo's golfing reputation was established on a global scale, and one of the favorite places for any international player to compete is the Australian sand belt. It is there that some of the world's most revered courses are found, chief among them Royal Melbourne. Faldo paid tribute to that sort of golfing experience when he designed one of the two courses at Wildfire Golf Club. At last count there were 108 bunkers on the Faldo course, and they are often arranged in imposing clusters. The ninth and 18th greens, placed close to each other and hard by the impressive façade of the JW Marriot Desert Ridge Resort & Spa, are surrounded by bunkers that come in various sizes, shapes, and degrees of severity.

There are plenty of bunkers to be found as well at the par-5 15th, the longest hole on the course and one that runs straight as a string along the edge of the property.

Two bunkers appear to the right of the landing area, but for the most part the first two shots on the hole simply call for solid strikes that stay out of the ever-lurking and unforgiving ground that occasionally makes up the most significant hazard in Arizona golf. It is the approach into the deep but skinny green that brings the player into contact with the traps. There are eight of them, one of which is a biggie that sprawls left of the green. Six of the bunkers run in a line beginning short of the putting surface and then advancing all the way up the right side. Given the shape of the green, plus all the sand, a precise effort is a must. It may or may not remind the player of Australia, but quality golf shots are usually rewarded no matter where they are struck.

Photograph by Golf Shots Unlimited

Publishing Team

PUBLISHER: Brian G. Carabet
PUBLISHER: John A. Shand
REGIONAL PUBLISHER: Marc Zurba
ART DIRECTOR: Emily A. Kattan
GRAPHIC DESIGNER: Morganne Stewart
EDITOR: Michael Rabun
DIRECTOR OF BOOK DEVELOPMENT: Rosalie Z. Wilson
ADMINISTRATIVE COORDINATOR: Susan Minner

Emerald Canyon Golf Course, page 55

INDEX

THE PANACHE COLLECTION

Dream Homes Series

An Exclusive Showcase of the Finest Architects, Designers and Builders

Carolinas, Chicago, Coastal California, Colorado, Deserts, Florida, Georgia, Los Angeles, Metro New York, Michigan, Minnesota, New England, New Jersey, Northern California, Ohio & Pennsylvania, Pacific Northwest, Philadelphia, South Florida, Southwest, Tennessee, Texas, Washington, D.C., Extraordinary Homes California

Spectacular Homes Series

An Exclusive Showcase of the Finest Interior Designers

California, Carolinas, Chicago, Colorado, Florida, Georgia, Heartland, London, Michigan, Minnesota, New England, Metro New York, Ohio & Pennsylvania, Pacific Northwest, Philadelphia, South Florida, Southwest, Tennessee, Texas, Toronto, Washington, D.C., Western Canada

Perspectives on Design Series

Design Philosophies Expressed by Leading Professionals

California, Carolinas, Chicago, Colorado, Florida, Georgia, Great Lakes, London, Minnesota, New England, New York, Pacific Northwest, South Florida, Southwest, Toronto, Western Canada

Art of Celebration Series

Inspiration and Ideas from Top Event Professionals

Chicago & the Greater Midwest, Colorado, Georgia, New England, New York, Northern California, South Florida, Southern California, Southwest, Washington, D.C.

City by Design Series

An Architectural Perspective

Atlanta, Charlotte, Chicago, Dallas, Denver, New York, Orlando, Phoenix, San Francisco, Texas

Spectacular Wineries Series

A Captivating Tour of Established, Estate and Boutique Wineries

California's Central Coast, Napa Valley, New York, Ontario, Oregon, Sonoma County, Texas, Washington

Experience Series

The Most Interesting Attractions, Hotels, Restaurants, and Shops

Austin & the Hill Country, British Columbia, Thompson Okanagan

Interiors Series

Leading Designers Reveal Their Most Brilliant Spaces

Midwest, Southeast,

Golf Series

The Most Scenic and Challenging Golf Holes

Arizona, Colorado, Ontario, Pacific Northwest, Texas, Western Canada

Weddings Series

Captivating Destinations and Exceptional Resources Introduced by the Finest Event Planners

Southern California, Texas

Custom Titles

Publications by Renowned Experts and Celebrated Institutions

Cloth and Culture: Couture Creations of Ruth E. Funk, Colonial: The Tournament, Dolls Etcetera, Geoffrey Bradfield Ex Arte, Lake Highland Preparatory School: Celebrating 40 Years, Family Is All That Matters

Specialty Titles

Publications about Architecture, Interior Design, Wine, and Hospitality

21st Century Homes, Distinguished Inns of North America, Into the Earth: A Wine Cave Renaissance, Luxurious Interiors, Napa Valley Iconic Wineries, Shades of Green Tennessee, Signature Homes, Spectacular Hotels, Spectacular Restaurants of Texas, Structure + Design, Visions of Design

Panache Books App

Inspiration at Your Fingertips

Download the Panache Books app in the iTunes Store to access select Panache Partners publications. Each book offers inspiration at your fingertips.